STEP UP & GLOW

Esther Gabrielle

Table of Contents

INTRODUCTION

Are you tired of looking boring, basic, and timid? Or you're looking for ways to boost your confidence? Well, this book will help boost your confidence and make you love yourself even more. Don't worry this is just a phase that everyone goes through in their lifetime. You just need to boost your self-esteem about certain things.

To "Glow up" means to improve on yourself and live positively. Nowadays we are all caught up with one or two things that we forget to focus on ourselves more. People tend to procrastinate a lot of things and just don't even bother about how they look throughout the day because we all just want to go about our day and come back home. Well, this book will help step up yourself and make you glow like never before.

Let's get started!

CHAPTER 1

Ways to lose weight with simple healthy

Okay! So, let's get started with our tips:

It's good to say that ladies are often meant to look good at all times. Not because we want to impress boys all the time but to see how stunning we look when we face the mirror. I know many of us like admiring and giving ourselves self-affirmation before we start our day. Likewise, before we head out to start our day you should consider doing the following routine to step up:

- When you wake up early in the morning try brushing your teeth as early as possible to avoid your teeth from becoming less whitened.
- I'll recommend taking hot chocolate instead of coffee due to the amount of caffeine in it.
- Take a shower. I always start my bathing with cold water and end it with warm. That way, it will help your skin glow better, and it's more relaxing to do probably when taking your mind off things in the morning.
- Find a skincare routine that suits you. For example, I use coconut oil and cocoa butter for my skin because it helps my skin glow more.
- Apply cologne. I recommend it better than perfume because the scent in cologne tends to last for a very long time than perfume.
- Have a killer style to wear out. You could get ideas from Pinterest if you ran out of ideas about what to wear.
- For breakfast you can try this any day you want: Pancakes, Fruit salad, Smoothie that contains a nutritional value (e.g. pineapple, mango, and

coconut), Fruit cereal, Green smoothie (e.g. lettuce, cucumber, spinach, and peas).

- Get a water bottle but instead of just water why not try detox water? Detox water helps cleans the system from dirt in the body. Detox water contains water, lemon, cucumber, and mint leaves). Squeeze the lemon into the water and then slice the cucumber inside it. Then add the mint leaves lastly.

When you try this routine out. Here's a chart to show how far you've gone within 1 month of doing this. You can start by writing how you feel now and after you followed my routine.

THEN	NOW

If you don't take proper care of your skin, then your skin might begin to break and may damage your skin. People tend to even deceive themselves when it comes to a skincare routine and exactly what the skin does not want, they use them all because everyone is using them. This is unacceptable. If your skin was perfect before you started using all sorts of things, then leave it just like that. Just stick to basic treatment that is suitable for your body. For someone like me, I don't have a skincare routine. I just apply baby oil to my skin to make it so soft and cocoa butter cream. That is enough for me. I don't outsmart myself and spoil my skin. Just make sure whatever skin care routine you use doesn't have any side effects but if it does, visit your dermatologist as soon as possible. Please learn to embrace your skin and it's okay to have pimples on the face darlings. We all will experience puberty.

CHAPTER 2

<u>How to lose weight with a simple exercise to do at home</u>

Finally! We are unto the next chapter. I assume that on weekends or holidays we always like to hit the gym to look drop-dead sexy or just to keep fit. But we end up not able to hit the gym maybe because of school activities, busy schedules or something just comes up. It happens to me a lot. Do you know what I did? I wake up 30mins before I start my day and do some exercise. I'm not into losing weight because I love my body the way it is. I just try and keep fit and make sure I don't have a big belly like that. Especially for those that hate belly fat, this tip is for you. Try this easy exercise:

- 10 pushups
- Bicycle crunches (1 minute)
- Scissor kicks (1 minute)
- Plank (30 seconds)
- Russian twists (1 minute)
- Dead bug (1 minute)

Within 1 month of doing this workout, you will get the result of it. I tried this same routine and I'm rocking these abs of mine. If you can do this from Monday all through to Friday and hit the gym on Saturday, you are keeping fit.

It's OK to look gorgeous and beautiful for yourself to improve your self-esteem. Remember that people don't define you, you define yourself the way you want people to address you.

I had very low esteem for my body when I was young. I always wanted to be skinny because I didn't like the way people just only complimented my body. I even wished puberty didn't even hit me that hard but I can't question my creator with the way he has created me. I always wore big-sized clothes and big skirts. I couldn't even wear bodycon dresses, trousers, or anything that will bring my shape out. The dirty compliments I got about my body were too much that I started to feel insecure about my body and didn't like going to social gatherings. Until one day, someone asked me why I hate going out and dress so shabbily. I told her because I was insecure about the way I looked and she said just one thing that changed my mind 'if you are going to let people's statements judge the way you act, you might as well just stay home forever and make your self-esteem lower'. Future me will want to be strong and brave and even advise others about their own lives. Ever since that day, I ignored people's dirty compliments about me and stay away from such people. By the time I was able to boost my confidence, IT WAS OVER for everyone that talked awful things about me. I started to slay in my way and dress comfortably. You see it wasn't very easy for me those times but I am grateful for the friend that helped boost my confidence.

You can even make up a workout routine that will be comfortable for you. But make sure they are not an easy workout but the ones where you can feel yourself burning some calories.

Note: After every 3 days of workout completion, try to take a break. I said so because? You might be stressing the muscles a little too much. So, after working out for 3 days on the 4th day take a rest and just stick to the healthy meal I've given you in chapter 1. See you in the next chapter lovelies.

CHAPTER 3

Ways to act cool and enjoy your own company

We are finally on to the next chapter!

If you haven't learned how to be on your own, walk to the coffee shop and have some alone time. Then you don't know how to enjoy your company. You need to start creating time for yourself and build your own happiness. Sooner or later, you'll realize you have no one but yourself. They are different ways to make yourself happy. Such as:

- Putting away your phone(seriously).
- Find something to do like starting a business that can earn you extra income to take care of yourself and glow.
- Bring a book or journal wherever you go. Just to scrap in something or even draw something inside. Just to keep yourself busy and feel less alone when with friends.
- Normalize doing an activity you love.
- Take a walk outside and relieve yourself from thoughts
- Take a warm shower when you feel things are not okay at that period. It's okay to cry if you have to. Crying can help relieve you from such pain at that moment.
- Go shopping if you have to.
- Get an emotional support animal e.g. dogs, cats

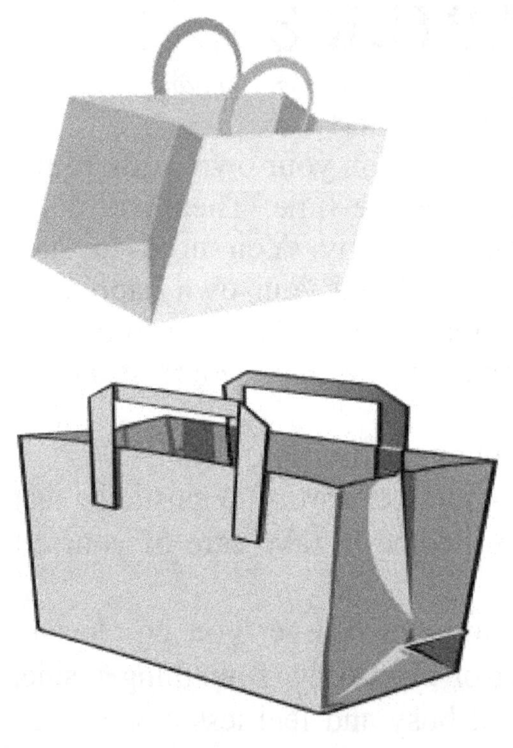

THIS IS A BLANK SPACE FOR DRAWING ANYTHING YOU LIKE

Being on your own can come a long way and you could even be making money while your other friends are partying their lives away. Remember to not force friendships with anyone. If you do, they could betray you along the line. We live in a life where we all face ups and downs. There's the good in the bad life and the bad in the good life. All these situations are what we will face in life. The road to a happy ending is never easy. We'll encounter circumstances along the way.

CHAPTER 4

Ways to improve your relationship or dating life

Welcome to the next chapter darlings!

A lot of us if not a lot, some of us have been engaged in a relationship while some haven't. For those who haven't been engaged in a relationship, we wonder what it's like to be in one. Honestly, it's amazing when it's with the right person. We all have someone we have had a crush on but don't know how to tell the person.

Well, it's not always easy for one to make the first move in a relationship because you're scared of rejection. The plain truth about this is even if you end up telling your crush about your feelings, whether he likes you or not life still goes on. Honestly, there's no shame in making the first move to a boy. There's always someone better that will love you if one guy rejects you.

Before we continue, give a response to this little survey

1. Are you in a relationship?

2. How has your relationship been with your partner this last few days, months, or years?

3. Where do you see your relationship going in the next few months, days, or years?

4. Has your partner ever beaten you?

5. Does your partner give you emotional anxiety or depression with the way they talk? (do they say things repeatedly to hurt you)

6. Do they do things you don't like intentionally or force you to do things you don't want to do?

Baby girl, if your answers are yes to these questions, I've given you. You need to leave such a relationship. It's because a relationship like this affects one's mental health and can affect your glow. A relationship is meant to be like a second home for you. It's where you are free to express yourself and not change who you are for your partner. It's important to always be with someone you are going to be comfortable with and enjoy their company.

There are some helpful tips you'll need to search for in a relationship:

- Someone who enjoys spending time with you.
- Someone that will go a long way for you to be happy.
- Someone who comforts you when sad

- Someone that will help get you tampons or pads instead of being disgusted because you menstruate or rant you out to their friends.
- Someone that cares about your opinions
- Someone that shows you love and affection

There are a lot of reasons to be loved and find yourself involved in a healthy relationship. But when being in a relationship, your relationship shouldn't be one-sided. Just because I said you should find someone with great characteristics that makes you happy doesn't mean you shouldn't show affection towards your partner. Try reassuring your loved ones that you love them. Reassurance goes a long way. People overthink a lot in a relationship and it's best to show each other the love and care one needs towards one another. In a relationship, if you lose feelings for your partner please always try to give yourself time and be sure about your feelings being lost. Sometimes, ladies tend to lose feeling in the middle of a relationship which is completely normal. It happens a lot. Probably, it's because you or your partner did something unattractive. But if you are sure of losing feelings for your partner, leave such a relationship instead of cheating and making your partner find out in a hurtful manner. Such a decision is very hurtful and unattractive. It's a very stupid idea to do such to someone that has loved you more than anything in the world. Learn to love one another no matter what.

CHAPTER 5

<u>*How to improve your communication skills*</u>

There are specific things to do that can improve your communication skills. An adage says 'Communication is the key to success in any business. Communicating can go a long way whether in sharing ideas or emotions. Here are ways to improve your communication skills:

- Listen. Listening to one another when giving out information to one another is very important. Important information that can act as an impact on your life can be passed, so it's best to listen when talking too.
- Who you speak to matters. Whoever you are communicating with matters a lot. Try communicating with people that will add value to your life and ignore the meaningless conversation. If the people you are communicating with are not adding income to your life then I don't know the kind of communication you are involved in.
- Communicating with body language: there are some situations where people tend to be in danger or an uncomfortable situation and can only conversate with body language. In such situations like this, try and help someone. You could save a soul when you master body language.

COMMUNICATION IS THE KEY TO SUCCESS

- Be brief and specific. When talking, try and go straight to the point and avoid saying irrelevant things.
- Write necessary things down.
- Think before you speak. Try not to just say things without thinking, you can look very dumb.

Sometimes, we get stage fright when standing in front of crowds. It’s not always easy to get over such fear but you should try to relax and take a deep breath. Another way to overcome this is asking your friends to help you, either by practicing in front of their siblings you have never seen before or their friends you don’t know about. Try practice with a nice stranger. Keep practicing till you are brave enough to talk to millions of people.

CHART BOX FOR PRACTICE OR TIPS YOU COULD PROBABLY WRITE DOWN FROM A STRANGER TO AVOID SUCH

Write a speech about how you would like to change the history of your country into a better one (650-800 words). After writing the speech, try implementing the steps I've given you

CHAPTER 6

How to improve on career advancement

Firstly, what do we understand by career advancement? According to google "Career advancement is the process by which professionals across industries use their skill sets and determination to achieve new career goals and more challenging job opportunities". The most important thing about a glow is making money. I know my ladies will want to make their dream life come true. The only way this can happen is to invest in yourself. They are so many career opportunities open to everyone. You can even take a job in the comfort of your home.

We all need money just to meet our needs. It's either we all want that expensive cars, the latest phones, have a luxurious house and wardrobe and a lot more. I won't lie, I want that too. Becoming that independent lady I always wanted to be has been my biggest motive and I'm sure it is for my queens also.

CAREER GOAL AND VISION: Where would you like to see yourself in the next 20 years? Write the obstacles you may face while achieving your goal and how you will tackle them

APPRECIATION

I want to say a very big thank you to those that took the time to read my book. I hope you enjoyed the book and it helped relieve you about some topics in a kind way. I'm really anticipating you guys' massive glow-up. Love you all, xoxo.

www.ingramcontent.com/pod-product-compliance
Lightning Source LLC
LaVergne TN
LVHW020547160826
845677LV00015B/4248
* 9 7 9 8 8 4 5 8 1 6 9 2 4 *